2/82

A

Follow a Fisher

THE FISHER'S RELATIVES

Mink

Otter

FOLLOW A FISHER

by Laurence Pringle
illustrated by Tony Chen

Thomas Y. Crowell Company New York

Badger

Ferret

Skunk

Designed by Karen Bernath
Manufactured in the United States of America
L.C. Card 72–83784   ISBN 0–690–31236–9   0–690–31237–7 (LB)
1   2   3   4   5   6   7   8   9   10
Library of Congress Cataloging in Publication Data
Pringle, Laurence P   Follow a fisher.
SUMMARY: Describes the domain and habits of fishers—weasels that live in North American forests   1. Fisher—Juvenile literature   [1. Weasels]   I. Chen, Tony, illus.   II. Title.
QL737.C25P74   599'.74447   72-83784
ISBN 0-690-31236-9   ISBN 0-690-31237-7 (lib. bdg.)

Wolverine

Marten   Weasel

About This Book

Fishers are big, beautiful weasels that live in wild North American forests. A few biologists have studied fishers, but their lives still hold many mysteries. About forty years ago, people in the United States feared that fishers would die out, but they survived and can now be found in fourteen states. Biologists and foresters have helped fishers by bringing them back "home" to forests where their kind had lived many years before.

I became fascinated by fishers several years ago, and read everything I could find about them. Luckily, it was also possible for me to visit forests where fishers lived. I followed their trails for many miles in the Adirondack Mountains of New York State, and learned something about their ways. Sometimes what I saw differed from the information about fishers that appears in books and magazines. When this manuscript was finished, it was read by Dr. Malcolm Coulter, Associate Director for Wildlife in the School of Forest Resources at the University of Maine. Dr. Coulter has studied fishers for fifteen years, and he suggested ways to improve the manuscript.

Eventually, some of the mysteries about the life of the fishers will be solved. Meanwhile, this book tells something about what we know of fishers today.

Baby Fisher

The weasel family includes some of North America's most beautiful and unusual mammals—playful otters, smelly skunks, graceful minks. Almost everyone has heard of others in this family—badgers, ferrets, wolverines, martens (or sables), and the little weasels themselves. But few people know about one of the most fascinating members of all the weasel family—the fisher. This big weasel lives in wild northern forests. It is worth knowing better.

No one knows how the fisher got its name. According to one story, pioneers in this country used fish to bait traps they set to catch animals. The bait was sometimes stolen by mysterious dark-furred animals, and the pioneers began to call these animals "fishers." Despite their name, fishers eat few fish.

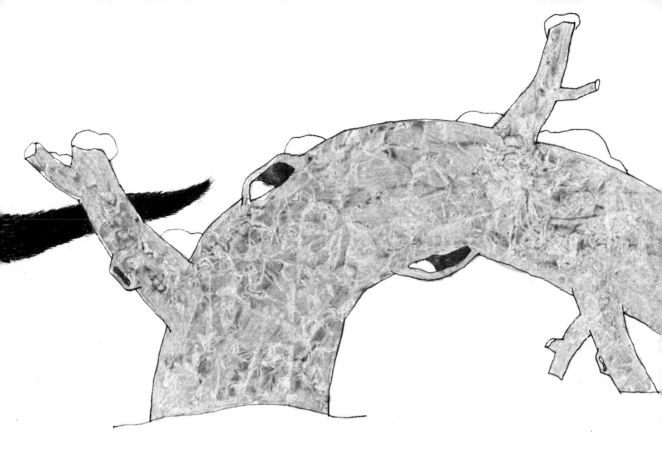

People sometimes call fishers "pekans" or "black cats." Perhaps the Chippewa Indians had the best name of all—*tha-cho,* which means "big marten." Fishers are about three feet long—twice the size of their closest relatives, the martens, or American sables. Like martens, fishers have short legs, long tails, and small, rounded ears. Female fishers weigh from three to seven pounds; males from six to twelve pounds. The largest known fisher was a male which was caught in Maine in 1963. It weighed twenty pounds two ounces.

The long, slim body of the fisher is covered with brown and black hair. The darkest fur is on the bushy, tapering tail; the lightest is on the head and shoulders. Males are often light brown on most of the front half of their bodies, while females may be glossy dark brown and black from head to tail.

Driving through the northern woods, people sometimes see a fisher cross the road ahead of their car.
The fisher quickly disappears at the forest edge. To
most people it is a mysterious stranger. But there is a
way to get to know this fascinating mammal: follow
the trail of a fisher in winter.

Anyone who follows a fisher trail is in for a day of hard work—and adventure. Imagine that you are in rugged Maine forest country, though you might also track a fisher in thirteen other states or in Canada. The snow is deep, so you strap on snowshoes. They are awkward at first, but soon you are moving along with big strides.

Then you spy some animal tracks. Pairs of footprints, side by side, mark the snow. Each print is three or four inches long in the loose snow. At the

front of each print are the marks of five toepads and five sharp toenails. You have found the trail of a fisher.

Follow the trail. In some places you will see that the footprints are close together—the fisher was taking small steps, moving slowly. In other places, each set of prints is three or four feet from the next—the fisher was bounding swiftly through the woods.

Fishers sometimes hunt in the daytime. If you're lucky, you may see a slim, dark creature run gracefully over the snow. But they are most active at night. In one night a fisher may travel a dozen miles. This fisher's trail may lead you up and down a mountain, across a swamp, along fallen logs. It may stop at the edge of a river, marking the place where the fisher swam across. However, fishers often travel along a stream until they find a beaver dam or other dry crossing. They seem to have regular routes through the forest. Every few days they return to the same ridges, swamps, and mountain ledges.

8

As you follow the fisher's trail, the tracks go from a hollow stump to a hole among rocks, then to a fallen tree. These are hiding places for animals that the fisher hunts. Then the tracks lead to the base of a tree. Here you find bits of bark on the snow. The bark was scraped from the tree trunk as the fisher climbed. Sometimes a fisher scrambles up a few feet and sniffs the air and the tree bark, searching for food—or he may look ahead in the forest. But this time, scraps of reddish-brown hair on the snow show that he captured a squirrel, then clambered headfirst down the tree and ate it.

9

Fishers are predators, killing other animals for food. They dig up mice, chase squirrels and hares, and sometimes even catch their swift cousins the martens. Fishers are also omnivores—eaters of both plant and animal food. They eat whatever is handy—a chipmunk, some berries, a dead frog, a nest of dormant bees. A fisher may spend weeks tearing at the remains of a deer, moose, or bear that was shot but not found during the hunting season.

Farther along the trail, you discover where the
fisher found more food. There is the mark of digging
in the snow, a spot of blood, a few short brown hairs.
The fisher caught a mouse. In another place you can
see that the fisher has dug up a store of nuts buried by
a squirrel.

The tracks lead on through the forest. Suddenly they veer to one side. Here are marks where the fisher dug deep into the snow. It dug down nearly three feet to the earth below, where a small spring seeps out of the ground. Nearby is part of a frog the fisher ate. Did the fisher smell the frog through all that snow? Or did it remember where it killed and left the frog months before? Perhaps this spring is a favorite hunting place

12

which the fisher visits often. There is no way to tell.

Now the trail you are following leads to a spruce swamp. Here the tracks change course many times, crisscrossing among the evergreens. They mix with the long hind footprints of snowshoe hares. Perhaps the fisher made a meal of one of these white hares, which bound through the snowy swamp like small ghosts.

13

You may lose the fisher's trail here. To find it again, circle the swamp and watch for the spot where the fisher left it. The tracks lead up a mountainside, to an area of rocky ledges and small caves. Here you pause to catch your breath and to look at the wild beauty of the rocks, snow, and trees.

Suddenly you hear a sound. *Unh, unh, unh.* It seems to come from high in a nearby tree. It could be the fisher you are following. Fishers sometimes make a low grunting noise. They also hiss and scream—especially when a bobcat or red fox threatens to eat their food.

15

Unh, unh, unh. You hear the sound again. This time you see its maker—a porcupine. It is chewing on the bark of a tree trunk.

Fishers often eat porcupines. Of all the predators in North America, only bobcats, cougars, and fishers dare to attack porcupines frequently. A porcupine's back, sides, and tail are protected with about thirty thousand sharp quills. When the porcupine is in danger, the quills on its body stand straight up and its tail lashes back and forth. An animal which attacks a porcupine may get a faceful of quills. It may be blinded. It may be unable to eat because of the quills that are stuck in its mouth and tongue, and may starve to death.

Many fishers carry porcupine quills within their bodies. Still, they go on attacking porcupines. Perhaps the quills do not harm fishers as much as they do other animals.

Some people claim that a fisher kills a porcupine by flipping it over and attacking its throat or stomach. This is not true. Fishers are strong, but usually are not strong enough to overturn a full-grown porcupine.

Only a few people have seen a battle between a fisher and a porcupine. The nimble fisher attacks the porcupine's head. Then it leaps away, beyond the porcupine's lashing tail. In and out, in and out dashes the fisher, biting the porcupine's head. When the porcupine dies, the fisher usually begins feeding on its underside, where there are few quills.

By attacking a porcupine's head, which has no quills, a fisher usually avoids being hurt. Fishers sometimes climb trees to attack porcupines that are feeding on bark or leaves. A big porcupine often weighs fifteen or twenty pounds—twice as much as a fisher. If a fisher can kill a porcupine, it has enough food to last several days.

Unh, unh, unh. The porcupine grunts again. It was safe in its rocky den when the fisher you are following passed by earlier. The fisher trail leads on up the mountain. You follow, and leave the porcupine gnawing on its tree.

The trail is straight and the footprints are far apart. It seems that the fisher was speeding toward some special destination. The tracks lead to the base of a maple tree, and no tracks leave. Scraps of bark lie on the snow. High up the tree you can see a hole in the trunk. It is the entrance to a hollow part of the tree that is the fisher's den, a safe place to sleep.

20

This den you have found is probably one of several the fisher has, in hollow trees or logs or rocky caverns. It may stay in the den for a few hours or a few days, depending on the amount of food it has recently eaten and on the weather. A fisher often stays in its den during a storm.

Fishers are usually wary of people, so there is no point in waiting for this animal to leave its den. Your tracking adventure is over—but perhaps you can follow a fisher another day. Later this evening, the fisher you followed may come out of its den, sniff the air, and set off on another hunt.

Biologists have learned about the winter foods of fishers by following their trails, and by examining the bodies of fishers caught by trappers. Once the snow has melted, however, it is impossible to follow a fisher's trail; and trapping is never allowed in summer. So it is harder to know exactly what fishers eat in summer. Since they are omnivores, it is likely that they eat some of the many different foods that are available then, including the eggs and young of birds, frogs, and berries. But their main diet is probably mice, squirrels, hares, and porcupines, as it is in winter.

Each fisher roams an area of ten or more square miles. Most of the year a fisher hunts alone—a single dark form bounding silently through the forest. Then, in March, the big tracks of males mark the snow alongside the tracks of females. It is the mating season.

A female fisher usually mates for the first time when she is a year old. The egg cells in her body unite with sperm cells from the male. The fertilized eggs develop for a few weeks and then stop. They change no further until midwinter, about nine months later, when they begin to grow and change again. The young fishers are born in March, about three hundred fifty days after their parents mated. This long period   23

of development, almost a year, is unusual for an animal of the fisher's size. It is equal to that of some whales and longer than that of humans.

The unborn young of martens, badgers, river otters, and some species of weasels also have a long, interrupted development, though not as long as the fisher's. Biologists are still puzzled about the reasons for this delayed growth of the young. In some yet unknown way, it probably helps the fisher and the other species to survive.

The baby fishers are born in a snug den. Usually there are three of them. Outside, the snow is deep and the temperature may be below zero. Inside, the young fishers are warmed by their mother's fur and nourished by her milk. At birth their eyes are closed. They weigh only an ounce or two. Their bodies are about an inch long and are naked except for some fine light gray fur on their backs. They make short, high-pitched cries, like newborn kittens.

In about seven weeks the little fishers can see, and they are now covered with dark brown fur. They begin to explore the inside of their den. They tumble about, play with bones and leaves, and fight over scraps of meat brought to them by their mother.

The female fisher cares for her young without help from the male. Soon after they are born, she leaves the den for a short while and mates again. The fertilized eggs begin to develop in her body, as before. Even as she cares for her babies in the den, next year's young are growing inside her body.

The young fishers stay in the den for about two and a half months, growing bigger and stronger. Then

they venture out with their mother, learning to hunt,
pouncing on small animals. Sometimes a little fisher
is killed by a great horned owl or other predator. By
autumn, the remaining young are nearly full-grown
and able to fend for themselves. They leave their
mother and go off to live and hunt alone.

27

Two or three hundred years ago, you could find the
tracks of fishers in many parts of North America.
When Europeans first came to this continent, fishers
lived in woodlands from one coast to the other, as far
south as Georgia and central California. They roamed
in forests where modern New York City, Pittsburgh,
Detroit, and Seattle now stand. When settlers cut and
28   burned the forests, the fishers disappeared. Forests

are the special living place, or habitat, of fishers. They depend on the woodland animals and plants for their food. Hollow trees provide fishers with protection from storms and enemies. Fishers could not survive where people cleared forests from the land.

As the years passed, fishers became scarce in many areas. In some states they disappeared completely.

Even in wild forests they were not safe from trappers. Fisher fur is made into jackets and capes. At times, fur buyers have paid great sums of money for the skins of fishers. This was particularly true during the 1920s, when fisher fur was very popular.

Sometimes a trapper would follow the trail of a fisher all day long. If necessary, he could camp overnight in the woods, then continue on the trail the next day. Eventually he tracked the fisher to a den and

killed it for its prized pelt. Trappers were especially eager to catch females, whose darker pelts were more valuable than those of males.

By 1930, it began to seem that fishers would be wiped out completely in the United States. Then laws were passed in several states to protect fishers from trapping. An unknown number survived, safe in their forest strongholds.

Before trapping was halted, few females lived long enough to raise many young. Once fishers were protected from trapping, however, they had greater

chance to reproduce and to increase their numbers. In the 1940s, about ten years after trapping was halted in several states, people began to notice that fishers were becoming more plentiful. They were spreading into forests where they had been wiped out many years earlier. The handsome big weasels became common in New York's Adirondack Mountains. They spread southward in Vermont, New Hampshire, and Minnesota. Between 1951 and 1960, fishers doubled their range in Maine. Trapping was allowed again in New

York and Maine, but trappers were permitted to catch only a few fishers each year.

In all these states, fishers were seen in country that had once been cleared and farmed. The farms had been abandoned when their owners moved to cities. Young trees had sprouted all over. Gradually, forests covered the countryside again. These changes took many years. The result was many square miles of new forests, and new habitat for fishers.

Where fishers increased and spread, porcupines became less plentiful. This gave some foresters and wildlife biologists an idea. They wondered if it would be possible to bring fishers back to places where they had once lived, especially to areas where porcupines were now common. When porcupines are too abundant, they do great harm to forests. Some trees die when porcupines chew away bark all around their trunks. Others grow poorly or become diseased after they are scarred by porcupines. In one year, a single porcupine can damage a hundred trees. Porcupines also damage other things—they chew on doors, wooden signs, automobile tires, and the handles of tools.

The foresters knew that porcupines were serious pests in some places. They knew that these rodents were so common because there were few predators to hunt them. Could fishers help reduce the number of porcupines? There was only one way to find out.

Between 1956 and 1963, about one hundred twenty fishers were let go in parts of the Nicolet National Forest in Wisconsin and the Ottawa National Forest in Upper Michigan. The fishers had been trapped alive in New York and Minnesota, then flown to their new homes and released. Actually, these were *old* homes for the fishers. When they dashed from their cages and into the woods, they were entering forests where other fishers had lived many years before.

Each of these fishers was marked with a metal tag in one of its ears. Soon there were reports that some of the marked fishers had spread fifty or sixty miles from where they were let go. And within a few years, fishers without ear tags were seen. They were the offspring of the fishers that had been released.

People noticed that porcupines were becoming less common. In Forest County, Wisconsin, an unusual benefit was reported by the highway department. A

few years before, porcupines had regularly chewed on wooden signs along the roads. Each year the highway department had to replace about thirty signs, at a cost of 25 to 40 dollars each. This expense ended when fishers returned to the area and the porcupine population dropped. The foresters were pleased with the results of their project. In 1966, they released fishers in the Chequamegon National Forest in Wisconsin.

Fishers have also been brought back "home" to parts of Montana, Oregon, and Idaho. They were flown to these states from British Columbia, Canada. Helicopters carried the fishers to remote places in Oregon's evergreen forests. Fishers from Maine were released in parts of Vermont where porcupines were damaging trees and property. Within a few years, foresters noticed that many porcupine dens were empty in these areas. There were also fewer complaints of porcupine damage.

So far, fishers have been brought to particular areas in order to be a help to people. However, there is another reason for releasing fishers in forests where they once lived. A forest is a community of plants and animals, in which each living thing has a "job" to do.

The fisher's main role is to keep down the numbers of squirrels, hares, and other small animals. A forest community is healthiest when all its members are present but none are too abundant. Fishers belong in the wild forest communities where they lived for thousands of years before people came to North America.

Wildlife biologists are pleased that fishers are thriving. Some kinds of animals have vanished entirely from the earth. Some of them became extinct even

before we could learn much about their lives. Other animals, such as cheetahs, blue whales, and bald eagles, are today threatened with extinction. The world will be a poorer place if these animals die out. Given a chance, perhaps they can come back as fishers have.

It is good to know that fishers are safe in their forest homes. Now we have an opportunity to enjoy the wild beauty of these fascinating mammals, and to learn the secrets of their lives.

About the Author

Laurence Pringle has been fascinated by fishers for many years and has learned something of their ways by following their tracks in the Adirondack Mountains of New York State.

He has written many informative books about nature for young people. In this book, his enduring interest in wildlife conservation and ecology has enabled him to supplement scholarly research with firsthand investigation.

Mr. Pringle was graduated from Cornell University and the University of Massachusetts. He studied journalism at Syracuse University. Another of his major interests is photography, and he has illustrated several of his books with his own photographs.

About the Artist

Tony Chen has been interested in animals since his boyhood days in Jamaica, West Indies. Included among his many pets were a goat, a donkey, and a young mongoose. His present home in Corona, New York, is once again the site of a private collection, but Mr. Chen's animals now take the form of sculpture from ancient China, Peru, Mexico, and Africa.

Mr. Chen's work has been exhibited in several one-man shows in New York City, and has received many awards. *Run, Zebra, Run,* which he both wrote and illustrated, was chosen by the American Institute of Graphic Arts as one of the best books of 1971/72. In addition to his work as illustrator of many books for young readers, Mr. Chen teaches drawing at Nassau Community College.